My Path to Math

GRAPHING

Penny Dowdy

Crabtree Publishing Company

Author: Penny Dowdy
Coordinating editor: Chester Fisher
Series editor: Jessica Cohn
Editors: Reagan Miller, Molly Aloian
Proofreaders: Crystal Sikkens
Project coordinator: Robert Walker
Production coordinator: Margaret Amy Salter
Prepress technician: Margaret Amy Salter
Logo design: Samantha Crabtree
Cover design: Harleen Mehta (Q2AMEDIA)
Design: Neha Gupta (Q2AMEDIA)
Project manager: Santosh Vasudevan (Q2AMEDIA)
Art direction: Rahul Dhiman (Q2AMEDIA)
Photo research: Sejal Sehgal

Photographs:
Alamy: Chris Howes/Wild Places Photography: p. 14;
    Dennis Frates: p. 18
Dreamstime: Rmarmion: p. 4
Fotofolia: Marianne de Jong: p. 12
Getty Images: Laurie and Charles: cover
Istockphoto: Christine Glade: p. 5; Iofoto: p. 7; Ivan Josifovic: p. 8
Q2a Media: p. 9, 21 (graphs)
Photolibrary: Creatas: p. 11
Shutterstock: Khokhlova Aleksandra: p. 10 (middle right);
    Apollofoto: p. 17; Gualtiero Boffi: p. 1; Dole: p. 20; Giraffarte:
    p. 6 (middle right and middle left), 10 (top and bottom);
    Anastasiya Igolkina: p. 6 (top and bottom); Joseph: p. 10 (middle
    left); Dmitry Remesov: (Mr. Jihn): p. 16, 19, 21; Taolmor: (Mrs. Tom):
    p. 16, 19, 21; Ali Varol: (Mr. George): p. 16, 19, 21; Vallentin Vassileff:
    (Mr. Turner): p. 16, 19, 21; Devochka I. Zaicheg: (Ms. Bates):
    p. 16, 19, 21

Library and Archives Canada Cataloguing in Publication

Dowdy, Penny
    Graphing / Penny Dowdy.

(My path to math)
Includes index.
ISBN 978-0-7787-4339-2 (bound).--ISBN 978-0-7787-4357-6 (pbk.)

    1. Graphic methods--Juvenile literature. I. Title.
II. Series: Dowdy, Penny. My path to math.

QA90.D69 2008   j518'.23   C2008-906088-1

Library of Congress Cataloging-in-Publication Data

Dowdy, Penny.
    Graphing / Penny Dowdy.
        p. cm. -- (My path to math)
    Includes index.
    ISBN-13: 978-0-7787-4357-6 (pbk. : alk. paper)
    ISBN-10: 0-7787-4357-8 (pbk. : alk. paper)
    ISBN-13: 978-0-7787-4339-2 (reinforced library binding : alk. paper)
    ISBN-10: 0-7787-4339-X (reinforced library binding : alk. paper)
    1. Graphic methods--Juvenile literature. I. Title. II. Series.

    QA90.D65 2008
    518'.23--dc22

                                                2008040148

Crabtree Publishing Company

www.crabtreebooks.com   1-800-387-7650

Published in Canada
Crabtree Publishing
616 Welland Ave.
St. Catharines, Ontario
L2M 5V6

Published in the United States
Crabtree Publishing
PMB16A
350 Fifth Ave., Suite 3308
New York, NY 10118

Published in the United Kingdom
Crabtree Publishing
White Cross Mills
High Town, Lancaster
LA1 4XS

Published in Australia
Crabtree Publishing
386 Mt. Alexander Rd.
Ascot Vale (Melbourne)
VIC 3032

Contents

Garden Center

Miguel's family owns a garden center. He is going to **survey** the shoppers. He will ask them questions.

He wants to count the plants people buy. He wants to find out if people buy more bushes, trees, or flowers.

◄ Miguel keeps track of his answers on paper.

Activity Box

What could you survey your friends and family about?

The garden center has
bushes, trees, and flowers.

Counting Plants

Miguel gets answers to his survey. The answers are called **data**. The data shows what kind of plants people bought.

He writes down what people buy.

Look at the answers Miguel collected. How can he make a **graph** with these answers? A graph is a drawing that shows the relationship between different things.

Customer	What plants did you buy?
Mrs. Jones	4 bushes
Mr. Carson	4 flowers and 2 bushes
Dr. Lin	2 trees and 7 flowers
Miss Becker	1 tree and 2 bushes

▲ Miguel's data looks like this.

The customers shop
for different things.

Picture Graph

Miguel decides to make a **picture graph**.
A picture graph has pictures that stand for numbers.
Miguel uses pictures of flowers, bushes, and trees.

Picture graphs have **titles**. The title of Miguel's
graph is "Number of Plants People Bought."
Picture graphs have **labels**.

◀ You can make picture graphs, too!

Activity Box

How many trees did people buy?

Number of Plants People Bought

How many bushes did people buy? The graph shows 8 pictures of bushes. That means that people bought 8 bushes.

Flowers   Bushes   Trees

More Counting

The garden center has bags of soil and wood chips. It has watering cans. It sells tools like shovels.

Miguel watches to see who buys watering cans. He sees who buys bags of wood chips or soil. He counts the number of tools sold.

This is Miguel's second survey. The answers are his new data.

Customer	What did you buy?
Mr. Dodson	1 watering can, 4 bags wood chips or soil
Ms. Greene	3 tools, 6 bags wood chips or soil
Mrs. Solis	2 bags wood chips or soil
Mr. Ross	1 watering can

The shoppers buy what they need.

Bar Graph

Miguel does not want to draw pictures this time. He makes a **bar graph**.

A bar graph has rectangles of different lengths. The length of the rectangles stand for different numbers. A bar graph also has a straight line called an **axis**.

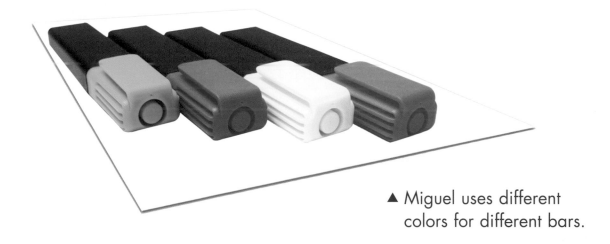

▲ Miguel uses different colors for different bars.

Activity Box

Go back to the data. Add the watering cans. Add the bags of wood chips or soil. Add the number of tools.

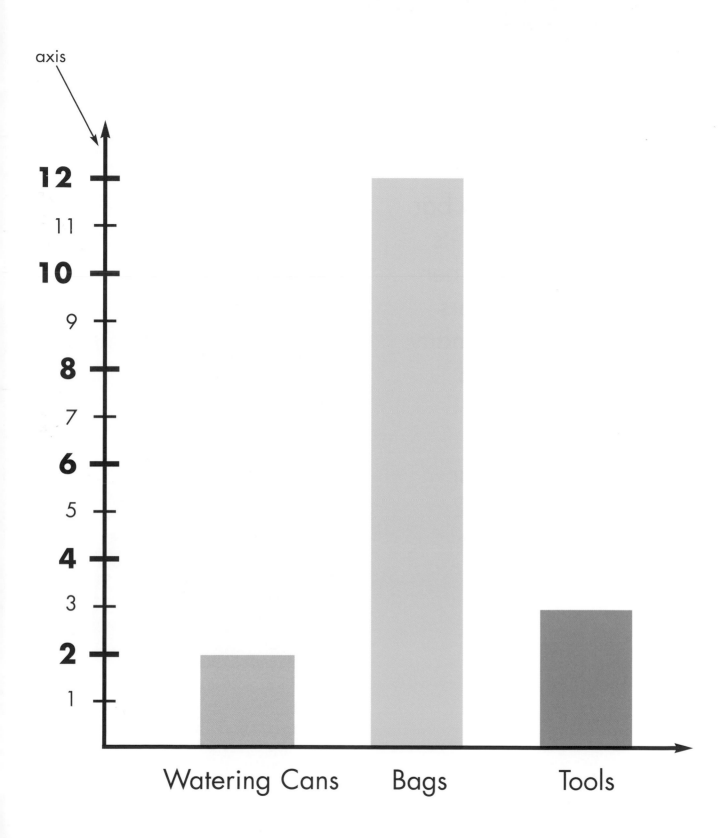

axis

12
11
10
9
8
7
6
5
4
3
2
1

Watering Cans   Bags   Tools

Here is the start of Miguel's bar graph.

13

New Answers

Miguel asks shoppers whether they bought plants or something else. He writes down the answers to his survey. He puts the data together.

The shoppers give him three different answers to his question. Some say plants. Some say they bought something other than plants. Some say they bought plants and something else.

Customer	Did you buy plants or something else?
Ms. Bates	Something else
Mr. George	Plants and something else
Mr. Turner	Plants
Mrs. Tom	Something else
Mr. Jihn	Plants

▲ Miguel's new data looks like this.

Who bought plants?

Venn Diagram

Miguel makes a **Venn diagram**. It shows a circle for each answer. One circle shows people who bought plants. The other circle shows people who bought something other than plants.

The circles cross. Answers that mean "both" are in the part that crosses. Miguel still needs a title. He can use his question for a title!

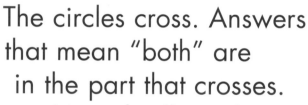

◄ Who bought plants? Look in the circle for plants.

Activity Box

Why does the middle show Mr. George?

Did You Buy Plants or Something Else?

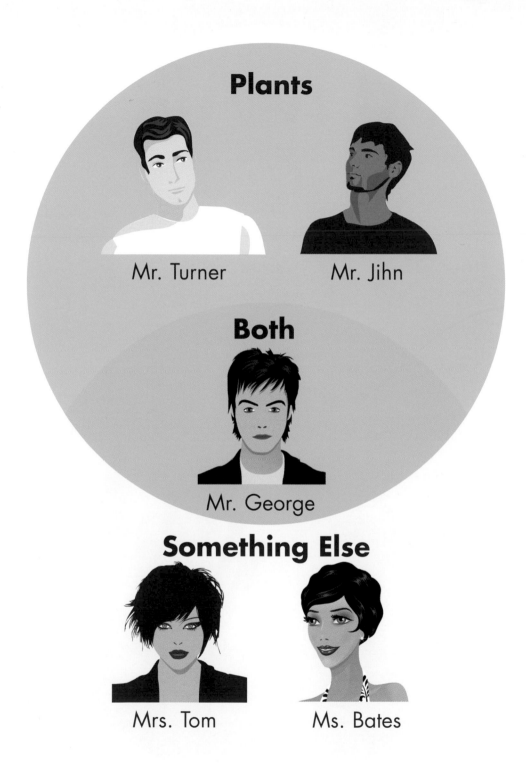

Plants

Mr. Turner   Mr. Jihn

Both

Mr. George

Something Else

Mrs. Tom   Ms. Bates

Here is Miguel's Venn diagram.

Seeing It All

We learned about many graphs! All graphs show data. Graphs make the data easy to understand. Graphs have titles and labels. They might also have numbers, pictures, or words.

Which graph used bars?

Which used circles?

How do you get data for a graph?

Number of Plants People Bought

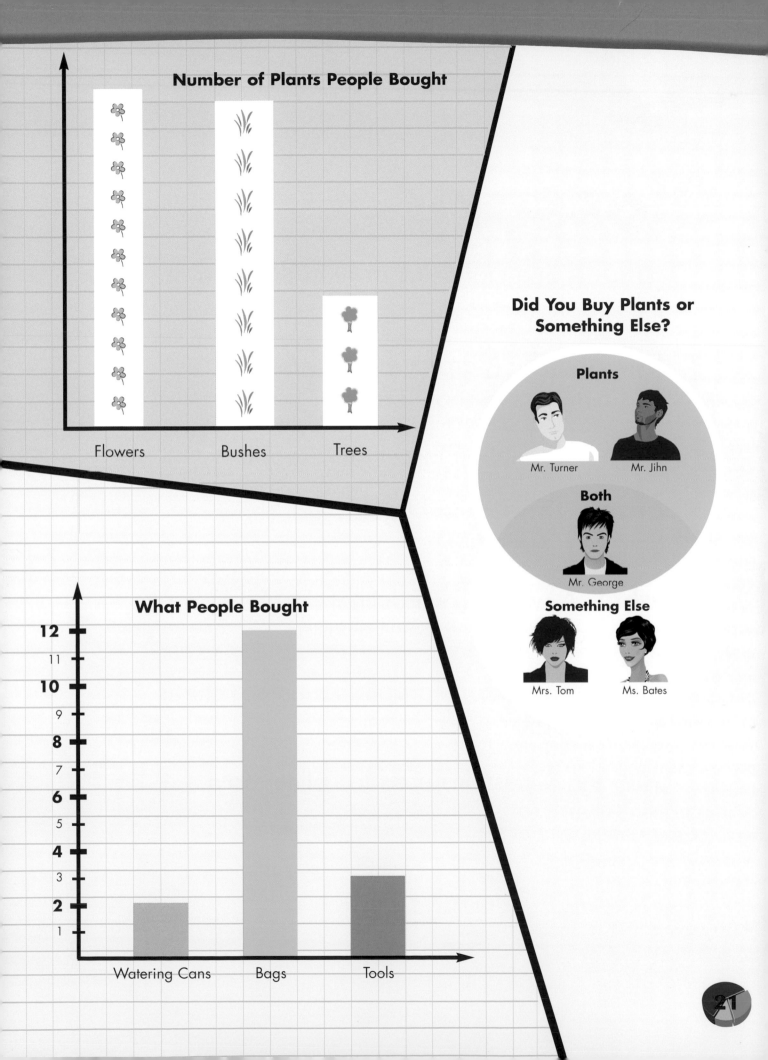

Flowers — Bushes — Trees

Did You Buy Plants or Something Else?

Plants

Mr. Turner   Mr. Jihn

Both

Mr. George

Something Else

Mrs. Tom   Ms. Bates

What People Bought

12
11
10
9
8
7
6
5
4
3
2
1

Watering Cans — Bags — Tools

Glossary

axis A line that helps us read the data on the graph

bar graph A graph that uses rectangles and numbers to show data

data Information to put on a graph

graph Drawings or figures that show data in a clear way

label A word or words that describe part of a graph

picture graph A graph that uses pictures to show data

survey Questions used to collect data

title A word or words that tells what a graph is about

Venn diagram A graph that uses circles to show how things are the same or different

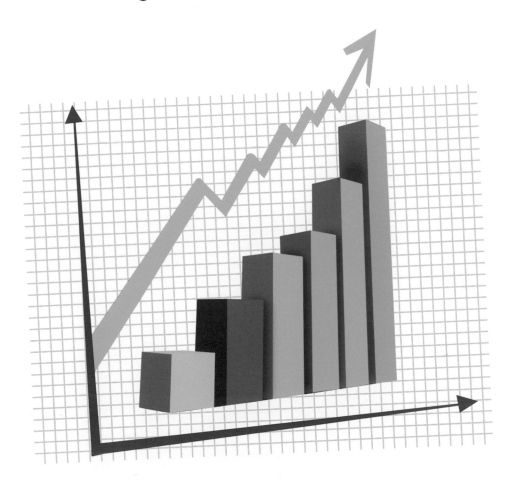

Index

Printed in the U.S.A. — CG